Gwyn Davies was brought up and educated in a rural environment and has a degree in modern languages. She spent ten years in cities in her 20s, seven of these in southern Germany, where she worked as a written translator for Daimler in the Press and Advertising section and travelled widely in Europe. She has a passion for nature and natural beauty and supports sustainable living.

To my mother, who knew many poems by heart.

Gwyn Davies

Moonshadows

Austin Macauley Publishers™
London • Cambridge • New York • Sharjah

A CIP catalogue record for this title is available from the British Library.

ISBN 9781398413924 (Paperback)
ISBN 9781398413931 (ePub e-book)

www.austinmacauley.co.uk

First Published 2024
Austin Macauley Publishers Ltd®
1 Canada Square
Canary Wharf
London
E14 5AA

Night Angel

Have you ever thought who's there
As you tiptoe down the stair
And see a slice of gold-bar light
In the middle of the night?

Breathing shallows, ice cubes cluster
Round the heart, enough for us to
Check our step and prick our ear
But not enough to freeze our fear
Apprehension quivers tight
In the middle of the night.

A ribbon breath of CO2
Squeezed in pain from lungs soon due
To collapse from lack of oxygen
Hovers, curls, ascends and then
Forms a question mark of fright
In the middle of the night.

Bony fingers clutching chest
Another step, I do my best
To keep my teeth from chattering

While heart continues battering
My rib cage with unholy might
In the middle of the night.

A creak, an arm jerks, both legs tremble
I know I cannot long dissemble
Who comes to isolate my fear?
The truth will creepingly draw near
Intruder? Demon? Whose cruel sight
Will pierce the blackness of the night?

One foot descends the stair, one hand
Clutches the rail like contraband
Transfixed, eyes peer around the stair
To capture the fiend in its moonlit lair
Horror, horror squeezes tight
In the middle off the night.

And that's when I know it isn't gold
But delicate moonshine, ephemeral, rolled
Across carpet and flagstone and garden lawn
A link with the night and the promise of dawn
Angel of promise, protection and light
Has come to give hope on the wings of moonlight.

And there by the fire, in the silver moonbeam,
Sleeps a child, head on fist, mind walking in dream
The bathroom door open, just slightly ajar
With its gold light cast slantwise in butter-block bar
But obscured by the power of the natural light
Of the kindly moon angel of silver night.

And as I look up, do I see one quick curl
And shimmer of gossamer robe unfurl
And barely touch the edge of night
As the dawn awakens to tentative light?
Horror no longer bonds with fright
To spoil the soft darkness of soothing night.

And now you know who will be there
When you tiptoe down the stair
And see a slice of cool moonlight
In the middle of the night.

Illusion

Have you seen the hand-sawn windows that I'm making for my house?
The work is delicate and costly and takes time
Have you seen the bathroom lighting, of a softly rosy hue,
From the lamps sunk in the ceiling, glow sublime?
Yes, I've seen the handmade windows and I've seen the lights aglow
But tell me, can you see the moon from here?
Can you breathe the cool, fresh air from the night winds blowing clear?
Can you see the moonlight shining on my brow?

See, I've stripped the plaster down and I've scrubbed the stonework clean
And I've rebuilt half the house, how hard I've worked
We needed much more room to accommodate us all
That's my duty to my kids – it's not been shirked!
Yes, I see the plaster stripped and I see the stonework cleaned
But have you climbed that hill right to the top?
Turned your face up to the sky, watched the feathered seeds blow by,
Sniffing pungent scents, from waving grasses gleaned?

Oh, I haven't time for walking, or for sniffing blades of grass
Such idleness when work needs to be done!
A full day at the office and then back home to work
If I want this house, I haven't time for fun
An hour's travel into work, an hour out again
And a day's grind in the city in between
Then it's home to planing wood and the knowledge, oh so good,
That we'll live in space and comfort, style pristine.

Have you never walked the singing woods in summer's dappled sun?
With the stirrings and the rustlings in the trees,
Or walked the darkness-coated hills and clutched at silver beams
Of stardust playing games along the breeze?
What price a life spent gilding rooms with no sight of the sky,
Confined by walls and ceilings deep inside,
When on your upturned face, fresh, cool raindrops down will race
If you brave the rain to hear the wet wind sigh.

So come on out along with me and leave the house behind
We'll cut our footprints in the crisp, cold snow
Through stinging rains and bright spring sun we'll tread the heather moors
And bask in summer sun's caressing glow
We'll cool our tingling fingers in sparkling summer streams,
Gaze from shady woods on golden harvest fields
And we'll feel the sweet fresh air in our gently blowing hair
And we'll merge our souls in heaven's bright sunlit dreams.

The Cake

It's calling me from the topmost shelf
The cake, I mean
You know what I mean

And lurking there with insidious stealth
The cake, I mean
You know what I mean

I'm sure it's watching me with mirth
The cake, I mean
You know what I mean

And laughing at my burgeoning girth
The cake, I mean
You know what I mean

But what I know it doesn't know
Is the picture I've put on the door for show
Which tells me how fat I'm going to be
If I don't stop scoffing the cake for tea!

Bliss

Your loving calms me like a tender blessing,
Enfolds me in such protective bliss,
My body wrapped up with your warm arms and legs,
My mouth claimed by yours with a kiss.

All softness my body floats, seeps into yours,
You give me such deep relaxation, such peace,
Such anodyne repose, the laws of love
They rule me, I have no defence.

The Rainbow

Sunlight, coloured sunlight casting
Spectrum of bright coloured shadows
Fading, fading,
Drops of moisture
Tiny prisms, throwing colour
Images, light water colours
Watered colours, bent by sunlight.
Climbing higher up the sky, they
Burst and bend into an arc.
See the splash, the shower of light,
The pot of gold the fairies conjured?
Sweep the sky, let me know,
How your colours blend and glow.
I cannot ask, until I die
How your colours form and why.
See the bird's wing trace the arc,
Chasing indigo to feel
The sweep of ecstasy within.
Gleam and blend and light the sky

Sweep and bend up there so high
You beam of colour,
        Fading now,
                Bright rainbow.

Velvet Diamond

The blossoming bough flows to the water's edge
Aimless, drifting in dreams
The water's soft current pulls at the dangling branch
And the soft swish of the waves
Reflects my silent thoughts

All that I have, all that I know
Is crystallised this moment
In the brilliance of this softness,
Like the starkness of a glittering diamond
Cushioned in velvet.

Ode to a Dictator

Hello "God", how's the world today?
How many victims have you hanged,
Upside-down, to pray?
How many do you keep
To kiss your muddy feet?
And why do you hang your ego out in front of those who weep?

We only see your profile,
Never the face complete
Show us the other side of your face
Go on – give us a treat
Go on, "God" – show us your face
Show us the other side
Turn it round and let us see
Your own satanic pride, "God",
The devil that's inside.

Christmas

Why has Christmas, come again
To this place of human pain?
Christmas stockings, Santa Claus,
Christmas trees and loud applause
For children's concerts, laughter bright
How can all this ease the plight
Of all who suffer, lost, alone?

But Christmas is for Christ to work his
Miracles through each of us.
Each time we smile, each time we give
Encouragement to those who live
In mires of fear and dark self-doubt
We work for Him and spread about
His love and hope and all the joy
Which those who live in Him enjoy.

The Christmas Biscuits

’Twas the night before Christmas, when all through the house
All creatures were crunching, especially the mouse
Who’d discovered the biscuits (who needs the cheese?)
But he breathed in the crumbs and this made him sneeze.

Up woke the master and lumbered downstairs.
“Who’s eating my biscuits? Who is it, who dares?”
A swirl of a red cloak, a flurry of white
Then silence, the jaws of the mouse clamping tight.

“My gosh”, said the master, scratching his head,
“It’s Santa who’s got me up, out of my bed.”
And grabbing the biscuits, he narrowed his eyes,
“It’s no wonder his waistline has grown to that size!”

Christmas Promise

A pair of hands that touch me lightly,
Resting on my head
Who'd have thought you'd still be with us
All these years ahead?

They say you were born in a stable
All those years ago
Years, or light years, time or light
What is time but a flash of light,
A mental fight to ignore in flight
Life's eternal glow?

How could a tiny baby,
A life in human form
Grow to encompass the universe,
The lightning out of the storm?

Do I believe it, do I believe it?
Do I believe what they say?
That He's always here beside me?
That He'll come again one day?

I am no dazzled shepherd,
No witness of Bethlehem's child,
Yet I know the living presence
Of that man they once defiled.

His breath blows in the breezes
And His arms wave in the trees
How could I ignore Him
When I'm faced with such as these?

His death is in the winter
But His life flows in the spring
To remind us of that baby,
That unearthly, earthly King.

Petals

To scatter petals on the sea
Like drops of pearls, sun-glinting on the waves
Would be to capture beauty's mist of gold
And let it seep into your soul's soft dreams,
Taking command.

Try to squeeze the tears from my heart
And watch the drops of blood
Like glistening jewels, dark red,
My life's colour flooding,
Like the sunset flooding Gethsemane
Burning Christ's body
And his blood flooding the naked Cross,
Staining the rough, wooden splinters.

Dead bones cannot walk, for the body's death is final
But the spirit must move on through mists of wonder
And the spirit's sensitivity is always alive
To the tingling of the sun's beams in the hazy heat
And the splashing of the waters to the river's white foam
In the half-light of the evening dusk
Under the stars.

A Night Snippet

In a ball of flaming fire
Burned the sun against a white-gold sky
With the Moon came peace
And a soft, caressing light against a cool, dark sky

Shredded, silver leaf patterns hover on my sill
Moonlight, day-bright, night sounds sharply shrill
Night air sparkles clear, sharp-edges sluggish vision
Now's the time to test one's thoughts
Now that night has risen.

Blood

Have you ever stepped in a pool of blood?
The horror, the shock, where is the body?
Who pulled the trigger, who drew the knife?
It's bound to be serious loss of life
Or could it be the gift of life
The silken flow of blood from the womb?
Or a gift from nature, rich, no worse
Than the silk from a silk worm or slime from a snail,
All part of the search for the Holy Grail.
But a pool of it, on the ground, brutal,
A harsh reminder of woman's power?
Her grim rejection of life itself?
Men, share in disgust.
No-one likes blood, wherever it comes from
Is it the colour, its stickiness, slime?
But red is so rich, its colour divine
In roses.
Sticky or textured, slime or silk?
BLOOD!
The threat of actual loss of life

If we see someone's blood, it's running out
But what about if it's pouring in?
Transfusion – filling life up to the brim
Why does blood disgust?

India

It beckoned her with jewelled hands,
That most exotic of far-away lands,
It entered her sleep and infected her brain
And she yearned to go, again and again.
But knocking on the window, knocking on the door
Came the spirit of disease and pain
And love was in there, too, of course,
Enveloping her common sense
For love, you know, is never love
But lust and aura, nature's way
Of keeping us here, the human race,
Just chemical ratios, all designed
To entrap us in the frenzied fever
Of producing the earth's new generation
So India was put on hold;
She'd go when this or that was done
And then, when it was eventually done
The money to get there was gone.
But India wouldn't go away,
Knocking on her eyelids, knocking on her mind
It beckoned her with jewelled hands
And she dreamt her way through sun-drenched lands

Through emerald-green jungles, where insects and snakes
Thrived in marshes, where boats plied their ancient trade
Carried spices and other goods, silver and gold
And jewels and silks and fruits too, untold
In their wonderful colours, intense and full
And deeply vibrant, and small, dark people
In bright coloured clothing worked.
But also the life-killing desperation
Of sifters and delvers in poisonous waste
Obsolete camels in impoverished deserts
The futility of the ancient spice boats
And majestic camels, all overshadowed
By the sky-surging, rearing, concrete and glass
Of the call-centres, giving the nation their jobs.
But still her mind was shot through with desire
For the great Himalayas, their peaks like spires
And the iridescent, piping birds
Flashing, half-hidden, through leaves and branches
And the lush foliage of that flower-scented space
Below in the foothills, where deciduous oaks
Flourish alongside pines and bush
And rhododendrons and rich-coloured blooms
Like anemones and blue poppies.
She dreamed of the house, precarious, built
On slopes, where houses ought never to cling
And Rajputs and Moghuls and Persian kings
Rajahs and Ranees and native princesses
Confined to exotic palaces,
Where fountains of water played in pools
And girls, dark and delicate, dressed in pearls
And delicate fabrics of turquoise and pink

With gold and sapphires around their necks
Dipped their feet in the water to cool their own heat
And hid from the sun.
And now she'd discovered the untold truth,
The truth of generations, stretching
Back in time, through the blood of brown girls,
Marrying soldiers, white-skinned, tall,
But most of all, these pale-skinned warriors
Loved them, didn't ask for more,
They were cherished and valued and when the men died
(As most husbands did, from heat or disease
In a climate their bodies were not designed
To cope with, their systems also not used
To the virulent germs of a different land)
They did their best to cushion their wives,
Their beautiful, dusky, generous wives,
From penury, but it could, nonetheless, not always be done.
So, seeing her line become white again,
This somehow gave her additional pain
And she wanted increasingly, more and more
To journey to that exotic shore
But her race was run.
Unable now to move about
The house became her refuge, draped
In scarlets and blues and silvery silk
And her bed the ultimate sanctuary,
Her place of dreams.
And now her spirit wanders free
And travels in India when she will
She visits the place of those desperate girls
Those love-sick, dusky, paler girls

Who finally entered the modern world
As white.
And what of the dark-skinned, original one,
An orphan, abandoned by all her kin,
Picked up from the step of a Christian church
And cared for, then married sensibly off
To a tall lieutenant, an Englishman,
Who loved her and lived with her many years
Before they both died?
No-one can know here but she will know
Now she roams the hills and the villages
Of that sun-baked, harsh yet enticing land
Of gossamer veils and silken folds
Of brilliant saris and tinkling bangles,
Bearded sadhus with mud-caked feet
And skin like leather.
Her dreams are ripples of shifting sands
Of the great, wide Ganges where all life's basic
Tasks are completed and people bathe
In filthy water and come out clean,
Where candles burn in empty shrines
And the destitute eat the offerings
Of food to gods.
She dreams of the widows, clad in white,
Abandoned by everyone, spurned and scorned,
Some mere children in early teens,
Never allowed to marry again, but shut away.
But the half-dusky/pale ones, they married again,
They were allowed a second chance,
Otherwise, she wouldn't have lived.
Yet with all its injustices, violence, hate

She is forced to concede that the melting pot
Of such an exciting, eclectic mix
Is an overpowering draw.
And so now, released from human pain,
She dreams her gauzy, tinted dreams
Of exquisite colours and siren calls
Of entrancing beauty and the burnt copper glow
Of sunset skies.

The Studio

Sharp-edged wire coiling me round
Manic twists of sudden sound
Whip, soften, yell and cease
From jarring stabs comes swift release
We're all intent, involved, amazed
(My shoulder twinges
I'd like some tea)
We're a team, collating each compact phrase
Shoulder aching, split-bone screw
Niggles persistent, squeezes sense,
Wrenched muscle tightens round the pain
Reminds me that of all my life
Much of it is past and gone
I'll never be young again.
Four bodies, tensing, facing front
Suspended concentration tight
Above them, caught in a twist of air
She's there, she's made it!
          A part of me
                    Instead of me
                              Because of me
She's out in the limelight glare!

The Elfin Shoemaker

Sitting cross-legged, head bowed low,
The elfin shoemaker crouches to sew
The leather he worships but never trades
And as the years pass, his youthfulness fades.

Day by day, year by year,
Crouched in his dark hole, his skin will grow sere
And his eyes, peering in the poor rush-light
Will grow dim and sunken and lose their sight.

He never sees the light of day
Incarcerated, he'd lose his way
If he ventured out, he's forgotten the sensation
Of the sun's warm rays and he's lost the temptation

To feel the cool fresh air on his brow
What would he do if he walked outside now?
His world has become his dark little cot
What happens outside its walls he cares not.

His privet hedge keeps him safe from outside
No prying eyes to peer inside
To penetrate his private world
To see his naked fear unfurled.

He's master of his own dark realm
He needs to stand alone at the helm
He stays up stitching all night long
Singing alone his shoemaker's song.

Who dares to buy their goods from him?
No-one is ever seen to go in
Who are his clients, and what do they buy?
From this world or fairyland? I hear the wind sigh.

Broken Glass

Words like broken glass
Fingers of flame
Reach out to smash and burn my hope
Rising to crescendo peak, then
Enthusiasm crushed by gods
Of ambition, faces of plastic teamed
With jogging suits.
Employment – that is all I want
Thrust in the gutter of residue slime
I'm washed away like fragmented trash
Splintered, cut up, body from soul
No one wants me, that's a fact
I'm even too old to appear on Page 3
(Not that that's been tempting me
But at least it's paid and well, I'm told)
I cannot quite believe my age
Mirrored in dreams of parchment faces
Rice-paper skin over china bones
Pale hair, ghost eyes, vacant and lost
My back is stiff, my bones are older
I've done too much and torn my shoulder
I need a job, to earn my keep

Not time yet to pack away self-respect
Give age a chance.

I run, tripping over my own lost hopes
Silent disdain in the eyes of the young
Isn't it time that I gave it a rest?
But I have no-one to insulate me
Age and experience do not sell me
The way they talk
You'd think that I don't want to work
They talk about encouragement
"Encouraging people to get a job"
I don't need encouragement
Bluster, bluster, government fluster
You've got it wrong, says my voice of dissent
It's employers who need the encouragement
To employ me.
Give desperation a chance, please
Give desperation a chance.

Honey Boy

With his handsome long tail and his honey-gold mane,
He's our own honey boy and so he'll remain
His velvety muzzle and gleaming white star
His whinny of greeting as he gazed from afar
Gold honey horse, gold honey boy,
Such a dear little horse was our Lenny.

We'll never forget him, he's eaten his way
Right into our hearts and there he will stay
Tail and mane flying, gold in the sun
Tossing his head as his hooves beat and run
He's still running with us, alive in our heads
Our Lenny.

He's just gone away to a happier place
To graze in flower meadows with the sun on his face
He'll be loved and looked after by others who care
And his days will be peaceful and forever fair
For our Lenny.

Running like an Engine

She's running like an engine
Swerving like a train
So bold astride her hobby horse
She's jumping in the rain

The buildings tower above her
They all seem far too tall
And she can't look over any walls
For she is far too small

And she must mind her parents
And do just as they say
She cannot do just as she wants
Their word she must obey

Then school and school and years of school
And then there comes the day
When she's at university
To study, not to play

And soon she has her own small child
Who's running like a train
And, bold astride her hobby horse
She's jumping in the rain

And she wonders what the pattern is
And where it all will lead
And what's the sense of human life
And what has she achieved?

And lying on her deathbed
The sense eludes her still
For all she's done seems pointless now
And her life seems bleak and chill.

For all the pain and suffering
The struggle and the strife
The hardship and the grinding work
Now cuts her like a knife

Why didn't she just go away
And linger in the sun?
And live off fish and coconuts
And live her life for fun?

All ye who labour now take care
You do not live to see
Your life evaporate in care
And struggle, endlessly!

White Ice

The lamp makes a shadow on the blank, white wall
But the shadow is still
A pair of shoes lies scattered on the deep, white mat
But the shoes lie still.

No human touch and no vibrations
To give this room life-warm sensations
And my heart is dying,
As my body, lying in this deep bed
Shudders and grows cold.

In this room where loneliness blows
In an ice-cold gust round my wide, high bed
I am isolated, feel no warmth
But the metallic glare of a white, steel lamp
And its light reflected from wall to wall
Each wall pure white.

I can see a picture on the wall
There are faces in it – human faces,
But the faces are dead, the eyes just glare
In one insane, metallic stare.

There are human beings in this place,
A human body in this room,
It thinks, it speaks, it moves its limbs
But there's no feeling there to bloom
In the pale cheeks or the hollow eyes.

Two bodies in the same cold room
No warmth between those human hearts
Hearts of stone, mechanically beat
But the mechanism soon winds down
And the heart stops, gradually loses heat
And the human body, growing cold, turns into ice.

Where is My England?

Finger-light touches and shafts of pure gold
Ripple and shimmer on pools deep and cold
And a kingfisher flashes, the bright turquoise slashes
Through air to dark water
His sharp beak pin-piercing
The water releasing
Him up with his wriggle-fish
Glint-wet to hold.

My feet long to wander down lanes of mud-dust
With hoof-prints and cartwheel ruts dried to a crust
And I'd even aspire to lanes of wet mire
For return of my England,
The freedom, soul-lifting
To wander, mind-drifting
In safety, without being
Knocked down and crushed.

Down leafy lanes, somnolent, basking in sun,
Where mice scuttle, chaffinches sing, rabbits run,
Where fresh green leaves sprout, then the year running out,
Glow in russet and yellow,

Where plants go unsullied
And wildlife unbullied
By fumes, pesticides and cars
But where's it gone?

Do we have more prosperity, freedom, more peace?
Where is the freedom you preach to me, please?
In my rural confine, my cramped limbs and mind pine
For the freedom to go on
Foot down country roads
Who wants to join loads
Of other cars, queueing
For space and release?

So gone is my England, its natural schools
Destroyed by blind greed of political fools:
Of perpetual masses with minds like crevasses
Of crude egoism.
As they grab short-term pleasure,
The green, living treasure
Fades painfully from them
Destroyed by ghoul rules.

The Spider's Web

He sits at the centre, spinning his threads
And weaving a web of intricate horror
Evil laced with the sound of good
Fanfares from trumpets of rotting wood.

They who sit round with glazed rapture
Written on faces of immature youth
Feel drawn towards the silken centre
Lured by the voice of the forceful pretender.

Too young yet to understand what they seek
In urgency or to understand
The urgency of what they seek,
These youthful pilgrims stretch out their hands

To warm them at the spider's fire
He holds their naiveté in his power
His listeners' slower brains are stung
By his lightning logic of two-edged tongue

His deviousness is so complete
That they're deaf to his own admission of it
They admire what they think is his honesty
Deceived by his pounding intensity

They listen entranced, agog for an answer
Not noticing that he gives them none
His words of provocative ingenuity
Conceal an abyss of horrific anarchy.

Their adulation feeds his fear
And dulls it, feeds his craving need
For adoration, for disciples young
To surround his pedestal in a throng

His whirling brain leaves them reeling, groping,
Confusion engulfs them and in their attempt
To understand, they begin to enter
The spider's web, and creep to the centre.

Into the spider's waiting jaws
And he will consume them utterly
He feeds on them to assuage his own need
Beware the spider's insatiable greed.

Grandsons

I'll give you a sweet if you'll get off my head
No, I mean it, I can't really breathe
And my lovely blue jumper is losing its thread
You will soon pull great holes in my sleeve!

Oh, no, not the arm pulled right tight up the back
That's not on, that really IS cruel!
I'll put you in prison, where it's cold and it's black
You'll have nothing to eat except gruel.

What? You'd like to see me get up out of this?
Is that what you torturers said?
That watching me writhing is hilarious bliss?
I'll have you both sent back to bed!

Ahh, get off my feet, I'm a poor old man now
How could you both do this to me?
What's that? You watched as I ran round the slough
And swam half a mile in the sea?

But that was two years ago, now things have changed
When you're my age, things change in one year
Help me up now and let me sit down in my chair
Get your grandad a glass and some beer.

Dear me, who'd have thought that two lively grandsons
Would make me a young man again?
I'm not, though, the ache in my body and bones
Is turning to actual pain!

I might never see them grow up to be men
But they're too young to take that on board
And as the years pass, I'll remember the joy
Of the tumbles and rolls on the floor.

The present is what life is really about
The way that we pass every day
It's important to savour the things that are good
Before they have all passed away.

Horrible Humanity

I was always taught to be
Sincere and loving, generous too
But daily more in life I see
Horrible humanity.

They steal the last spoonful of jam in the jar
They tread on your heels in the queue
They try to ensure that no beer in the bar
Goes to someone as patient as you

Six-footers peer over your shoulder
At every known hole-in-the-wall
To add to their database folder
Your pin number, details an' all

They squeeze you right out of the one parking space
By parking just over the line
They've no right to park *there*, but the playground is full
And for schoolkids it's going-home time.

Do you think their kids could walk, just around the block?
No chance, the sudden exercise could prove too great a shock!
Where have all the manners gone
Short time passing?
Where has all the patience gone?
Wasn't ever there.

All of us are what we are, intent on our surviving
By whatever means should come our way – cunning and conniving!
Push the other out the way
Selfishness has won the day.

That green-eyed monster's lurking there
And rolling those big eyes,
Fluttering those lashes
          Rolling cumbersome hips
                    Beckoning with mottled fingers…

                    In order to devise
                    This selfish hatred man-to-man
                    She only has to beam a glance
                    Of green fluorescence, spin a dance
                    Before our eyes, so hypnotised
                    And we will
                              Fall,
                                        Fall,
                                                  Fall.

Reality

I'm taking steps towards my death
Haunted by a spirit, evil,
Whirling round me with its shroud
To wheedle this one from the crowd
To trap me in my own fear's making
Is the evil also of my making?
Insanity's dark cobwebs weaving,
Spreading through my brain and leaving
Traces of a coal-dust darkness
Is it darkness that I see?
Or is it my reality?
My eyes see blackness, but it might
Be that which others seek to fight
Or yet which someone else's sight
Sees as daylight, not as night
Dark fingers, pushing upwards try
To smother reason, as I lie
Beneath the threat of pressing blackness
Panic edging nearer, pushing,
Tries to topple me and I am
Fighting, fighting, fighting what?
My own fear of I know not what

Fear of worlds I know not where
Worlds, what worlds, what is out there?
Out where? The boundaries are blurring
Nothing's fixed and in my head are whirring
Wings of bat-like, frenzied beating
Beating out my shreds of reason
Reason drops into confusion
Reason, what is that – illusion?
Limits, boundaries, they blur
I know no limits anymore
I'm clinging to what my eyes see
Another's unreality?
What evil haunts me, fills my mind?
What evil claws are set to grind
My reason down to dusty madness
And oh, this dreadful, dreadful sadness
My spirit wanders, hopeless, lost
No direction, pain-tossed,
Love skewered on knives of pain
Will I ever guide myself again?
Or will I always haunt these mists
And merge from day now into night
Or will I enter into light
And do I know that light exists?
There's only one thing that I'm sure of
Only one thing that I know
While I am mortal, drawing breath
I'm taking steps towards my death.

The Old One

We lived with a ghost for 20 years
You can't have, spirits don't exist
Except they do in your cupboard, mate –
What have you got in there – whisky, gin?
How much have you had today?

Nothing yet – it's breakfast time!
None of your business, anyway
Mind my feet, you clumsy oaf!
You were telling me about the ghost,
Oh, look at your pants on display!

Please *don't* shake my hand, I always say,
But do they listen, none of them do,
Eh, what have you brought me in today?
Not a *tin* of peas, I said a pack,
Those ones in the tin taste like dust.

Anyway, just look at this cloth,
It's filthy, it's going in the wash,
I'll find another; well, make sure you know

Where all the things go, then,
And put them all back as they were.

You were telling me about this ghost,
What? You were saying when I came in,
Oh yes, well I said so because I heard
A noise on the staircase before you appeared
That's just how it happened before.

Well, what's it like then, does it speak?
Does it stand there all white with staring eyes?
Don't mock me, mate, I know what I heard.
Well, what does it look like? Tell me then.
It doesn't *appear,* I just hear!

Well, that could be anything, couldn't it?
Of course it couldn't, sounds don't just occur
For no reason, and who else is living here?
Well maybe you should limit the gin,
Listen, mate, I don't *ask* the thing in!

Well, I'm going in the kitchen now
To make you a drink and put these away
If I see the ghost I'll sound the alarm,
Silly old buffer's imagining things,
That's what it's like when you're old.

I won't be a minute, where's the biscuit tin?
Tea or coffee, what do you want?
Hey, Charlie, I'm asking you, what do you want?

He won’t speak to me now, he’s taken the hump
Here, I’m bringing it in then, it’s tea.

Charlie, Charlie? You’ve not gone to sleep?
I don’t believe it, he has, he’s gone off,
But his eyes, they’re open and staring at me!
Hey, close your eyes, Charlie, I can’t bear that look,
It’s boring right into my head!

There’s the doctor, he’s ringing the bell,
He’s in the back, doc, dead to the world,
Oh, sorry, I didn’t…but he is, I think,
You’d better have a look yourself,
I’ll make us a fresh cup of tea.

I’ll go in the kitchen and leave you alone
He was telling me about this ghost
But I didn’t care, I was making the tea
And…did you hear that? Hear what? That sound…
What’s that sound I hear on the stair?

Watch Your Step

I'm going up a ladder steep
Must make sure that I watch out
Must wear the regulation shoes,
The recommended safety shoes,
Not slip-on shoes that let my feet, my funny feet, fall out.

Oh, now there's someone at the door
I'm already half-way up
So, up or down, which way to go?
Have they seen me? I don't know.
I'll stop a moment, half-way up and let my thoughts take shape.

I want to clean the top bookshelves
Which I need to do today
Not take time off for visitors
But still, I don't know who they are
So better go back down again before they go away.

Oh, now I see there's no-one there
And I have come back down
So now I'll have to go back up
And the phone rings when I'm half-way up
So should I answer it or not? I'm practically atop!

And the third time I ascend the rungs
And reach the ladder top this time
I realise the kettle's on
The tiny kitchen's full of steam
So I must come back down again and just renounce my dream.

My dream of having clean bookshelves
What does it matter, anyway?
While I was up there I observed
A book I haven't read in years
A record of my youth and age and many hopes and fears.

A diary-with-the-photos book
A record of my life and work
And other books are up there too,
And maybe I could take them down
And, taking them in order, I could read them all again.

So the ladder goes away again
And the regulation shoes come off
I make my way towards my chair
And, bending forward, books in hand,
I catch my foot inside the leg and crash upon the ground.

Some books went with me to the ward
Someone put them in my bag
And there's time enough in hospital
To read them one by one
And when I get back home again, I'll wipe the bookshelves clean!

It's safer climbing ladders
Than lugging books about
Because one's focussed on the job
And not on reading all the books
One takes from all the bookshelves when one wants to wipe them clean!

Heaven and Earth

A lone bird soared into the milk blue sky
And, its curved wings forming a line to join the sun,
It drew towards it every human eye
That ever longed such freedom to have won
But freedom so profound, man can't possess
His calculations bind him with his brains
His complex mind and life allow no rest
And instead of liberty, he walks in chains
He sees the shimmering mountains touch the skies
And throw their darkening shadow o'er the sphere
He bows his head to earth with doleful sighs
And goes on trudging, drudging, year by year
He looks to heaven to tell him he is right
But shrivels in the nothingness of night.

War

The war clouds gather again, yet again
In a painful wave of inspiration
I know that this will never cease
And the battles will rage on.
Death comes from the old
Shall death come to the young?
Ancient warrior shakes hands with modern gunman
Tristesse.
The slickness of superficial calmness
Reflects the core of hidden hardness
Despair
In every heart that is no heart.
No purity, no simplicity, confusing complexity.
Vitality is stifled under barrage of questions
Which chase, chase and forever chase
In desperate search of answer.
Arrows pointing, knives chopping, guns vibrating –
Vibrations wrenched from the dead man's body
Anguish
A word no longer with meaning

Obsolete, the street-man calls it
It has no meaning, it has no feeling,
It crashes against a hard wall of deadness,
Of numbness, of denseness, of senselessness
Of War.

Mother

Gone, but not lost, your presence still there,
I know you're around me, dancing in air,
No longer confused, or unsure, or fraught,
The breeze brings your voice, full of love and support.
The night brings your shadow, the day brings your face
Smiling now, tender, watching my pace
You walk along with me, steadily now
On paths we both loved, where summer winds sough
And the trees bend to meet us and wild flowers bloom
And we'll both be together and you'll welcome me, soon.

Youth, Lost and Gained (A Sonnet)

Harsh wind, vicious, rips out roots
Of withered, weary trees
And flings them spitefully amid green shoots
Of new life, springing, she's
The green goddess, hallucinatory, cruel,
Her aim to mould one's mind
Into enslavement, trapped beneath her rule
To corkscrew twists, the kind
Whose dark torment heaven's brightest gleam won't light
She kills the strength to fight.
But all the roots are not quite dead, not quite
An old one thrusts out new
A fine green shoot, to blossom in sunlight
With strength, serene and true.

Strange Spirit Walking Crooked Roads

All you leaves, so brightly green, rustle in the wind
Flurry, flurry, flurry, you rustle in the wind
Such delicate, finger leaves, bend from right to left
As the strong wind, the bold wind whips you with his breath
But you slip back, you spring back, your stems he cannot break
Your fresh green sap will push you back to flutter, not to quake.

All you ears of barleycorn, you whisper in the wind
Heads bent low, moving now, you whisper in the wind
Your stems, they shake and quiver as your ears lift to the breeze
And the corn takes on a sun-ripe hue, gold against green trees
They'll cut you down and harvest you when you're ripe and dry
But short-lived though your beauty be, it's stamped upon his eye.

All you mountain becks and burns, you foam and splash and rush
You hurl white waters onward in a whirling splash and rush
You stop for nothing, rock nor tree may halt your surging course
As you hiss and foam and bubble, taking obstacles by force
Downward dive, swift current strive, path carving to the sea
Fresh waters meet with salty wash and mingle, carelessly.

Cascading waters, rushing winds, fluorescent, dancing leaves
They beckon him, enticing him, entrancing, dancing leaves
Strange spirit walking crooked roads, he follows where they lead
Where beauty calls to him, along that pathway he will tread
No straight road will he trudge along with blinkers on his eyes
But you'll see him in the distance, chasing shadows, fooled but wise.